Learn How To Make Micro-Macrame Jewelry Volume 2

By Kelsy Eason

Table of Contents

Tools	6
The Essential Project Board	8
Cords & Beads	11
Basic Knots	13
Project 1 - Summer Sunrise Earrings	33
Project 2 - Meandering Brook Bracelet	41
Project 3 - Wild Cinnamon Fern Bracelet	54
Project 4 - Island Cove Necklace	71
Project 5 - Lacey Sea Coral Bracelet	86
Project 6 - Pizzaz Anklet	104
Project 7 - Micro Macrame Cross	112
Tips	67
Gallery	68

Introduction

Learn How To Make Micro-Macramé Jewelry!

Volume 2

Intermediate / Advanced Designs

Learn to create Micro-Macramé beaded jewelry with these 7 fun projects.

My previous book, "Learn How To Make Micro-Macrame Jewelry! Volume 1", explained how to create the necessary padded work surface which allowed you to embark on your micro-macramé journey. Then we continued with a straightforward bracelet, enabling you to familiarize yourself with the feel of the cord giving you time to practice tension as you tie the most commonly used knot in micro-macramé. Each successive pattern introduced you to a new knot or two, culminating in a final project using several knots. If you are new to Micro-Macrame, I would suggest starting with my first book before you move on to these patterns.

In this second book, I wanted to move forward into some more advanced techniques and knots. I've added some new knots and have increased the complexity of the designs which really brings you into what I enjoy the most about the craft. That being the intricate details and delicate beading which sets apart this style from other forms of jewelry making. My approach is even different from many other knotting trends as I lean towards the Margarete Lace (or Margaretenspitze) technique.

I've included the project board design, basic tools, cords, beads and basic knot information at the end of this guide for easy reference.

With just a little practice you can learn how to create even more advanced designs.

For more patterns, visit my website at www.demure-designs.com. I'm adding new designs all the time.

Included Projects

In this guide, you will find the following projects.

Summer Sunrise Earrings

Meandering Brook Bracelet

Wild Cinnamon Fern Bracelet

Island Cove Necklace

Lacey Sea Coral Bracelet

Micro Macrame Cross

Pizzaz Anklet

Tools

Reaming tools

Beautiful beads can really complement your project. What fun it is finding that just right shape and color, then rushing home to work it into your creation – and what disappointment if you then spend hours wrestling with the tiny bead opening which is stubbornly refusing to go on to your cord.

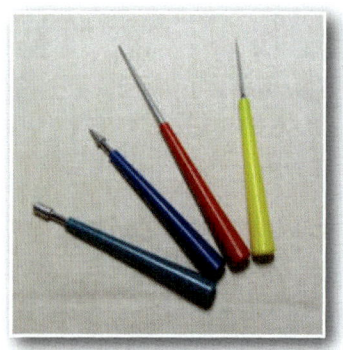

So what is the solution? A simple set of bead reamers. I purchased a set of four reamers, each of various size. Most often used is the smallest, but I have had occasion to reach for the next size up also. My reamers are for use on glass, ceramic and stone beads. This tool has truly smoothed the way with tricky beads.

Beading tools

It is a good idea to have basic tools such as crimpers and needle nose pliers on hand. Several patterns have jump rings or ribbon clasp closures which would benefit from the use of such tools. You will also need a set of small, sharp scissors to trim cords.

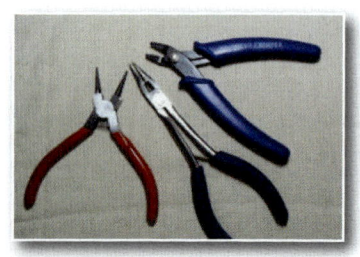

Glue

Often in micro-macramé, your only loose ends are at the end of the project when you tie it all off. In my experience, this is your weakest link. So why not strengthen it as best as you can? It is important to seal these ends so they don't unravel. Many people use nail polish; I prefer glue. One of the popular crafters clue is GS Hypo Cement.

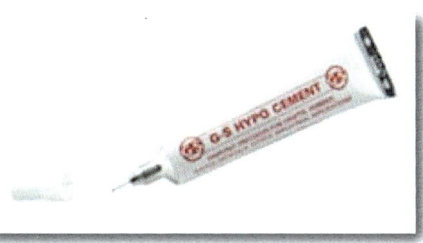

Personally I use a generous amount of Beacon 527 multi-purpose glue. It dries clear, though shiny. Usually I leave it to dry well (often overnight) then trim my cords and apply a second coat. Some use a singeing tool to fuse the ends of nylon cords, melting them together. This leaves a bit of black residue, so use only on dark cords.

Pins

Straight pins are significant in micro-macramé design work. Some people prefer T-pins. Either way, a long shank is more comfortable to work with. Pins are vital when it comes to holding cords in place, and invaluable for teasing out a mistake without unraveling your cord.

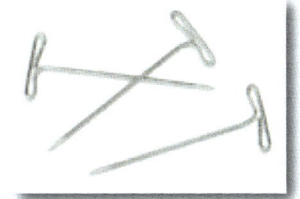

The Essential Project Board

There are several different kinds of padded board designs available on the internet. Some are made of foam and others of cork. When creating mine, I made sure to use thick foam which gives me the ability to push my straight pin all the way in, using the head to hold the cord tightly when necessary. A feature I used often when I was first learning.

To make my board, I started with a leftover piece of foam that was lying around. (Ok, it was lying around at my mom's house, but it was in the attic, so it's fair game, right?) As you can see I made a rough cut that is actually a bit larger than my clip board. This is about 12in x 13in.

Then, where the top clip will be, I cut out a slope. This is to help the foam to slide under the clip.

Next I added about 4 inches to each side and cut out my fabric. Choose wisely here. On my first try I used a very light, soft pink fabric that was a flannel type of material. When I worked on a project though, especially picking up beads to string onto the cords, I was forever having little bits of fluff on my fingers and in my way. Pick something with no "pilling" ability.

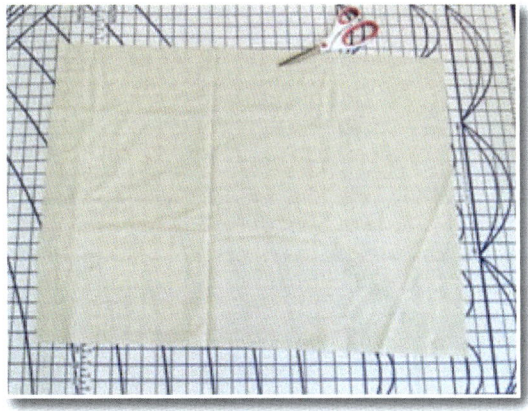

Cover the foam with your fabric. Turn to the back and safety pin it in place. I like to be able to take the cover off to wash it (there may be a coffee spill in the future) or just change it out if it doesn't work (like the aforementioned pink stuff).

Turn to the front and fit onto your clipboard.

I keep straight pins in the top corners of my board, which I use to pin cords, hold the fastenings (closures), or keep a focal bead for later use my current project. The only negative I have found with this design is that if I have loose beads on my board and I move the board, those beads inevitably roll right down against the clip. The good news is that I always know where they are!

Cords & Beads

Types of cording

C-Lon - My patterns use a cord called C-Lon Bead Cord. It is a 3 ply nylon cord comparable to Conso and Mastex Nylon #18, but offers a much larger range of color options and a smaller price per spool. This cord is the standard size for micro macramé jewelry. It is also available in smaller diameters such as C-Lon Micro Cord and C-Lon Fine Weight Bead Cord.

Tuff - Also a 3 ply nylon cord, it is available in 16 colors and has several size options. It doesn't stretch or stain, and resists fraying. Size 5 is comparable to C-Lon Beading Cord.

D&E (formerly Mastex no. 18) – nylon cord originally designed for the upholstery industry, it is soft and pliable. Available in about 17 colors.

Types of beads

Metal – These are non-precious metals which offer a less expensive alternative to silver and gold.

Crystal – It is the refraction created by the many cuts in a glass surface that gives crystal it's fancy shine.

Glass – This category is where you will find flame work and lampwork beads.   Versatile and affordable, glass bead are an excellent choice for novice beaders.

Semiprecious (or gemstone) – These beads are a popular choice as they offer a large variety of options. The list is extensive, so here are a just a few: agate, amber, garnet, jade, malachite and onyx.

Clay - These beads can be made of ceramic clay, which is fired in a kiln and glazed, or made of porcelain which generally involves a potter's wheel, a kiln, and hand painting. There is also polymer clay which is not technically a clay at all, but a plastic. This material is an oven- baked clay that can be used at home to make your own unique beads and is very versatile.

Other - There are also beads made from shell, such as mother of pearl, tiger shell, abalone, and conch shells. You may also come across wooden beads which come from the bark, roots or branches of many types of trees. Some wooden beads are carved and have been popular for generations.

Basic Knots

Now let's get into the heart of things. Here are the basic knots for micro-macrame shown in step-by-step format. Refer back to it when you begin your project. Don't get overwhelmed… with just a little practice, you may be surprised at how quickly you pick up these techniques.

Lark's Head Knot

Fold your cord in half. Take the loop and fold it over whatever you are attaching it to. Front to back as shown.

Take the two cords that are dangling in front and feed them through your loop so it looks like this:

Page 13

Now just tighten it up.

The Lark's head knot is great for attaching cords to key rings, a donut bead or a slider bead. You can also use the Lark's head to secure your cords onto a watch face to create a band.

Overhand Knot

Your basic tie-your-shoe knot.

Flat Knot (aka square knot)

This is one of the most popular knots in micro macramé. You can work the knot beginning with either the right cord or the left. I usually begin with the left cord. It is most often worked using two outer cords and two or more inner or filler cords.

Place the left cord over your filler cords. Then place the right most cord over top of the left cord.

Take the right cord and move it under your filler cords, then out over the left cord.

Since we worked the first half of the knot with the left cord, we now begin with the right. So place the right most cord over the filler cords. Then put the left cord over top of it.

Run the left cord underneath the filler cords and out over the right cord. The picture shows what the cords look like, however you will want to tighten the first set and then snug up the second set.

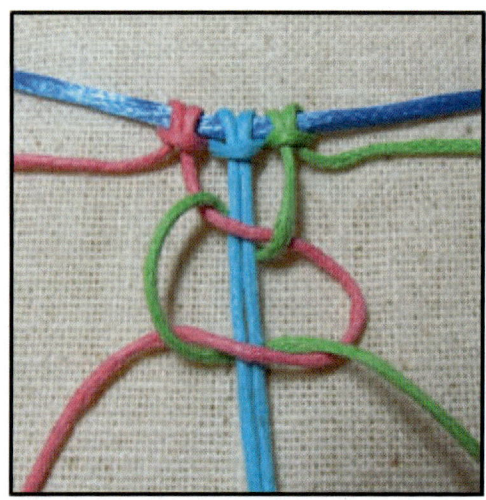

Here is the full flat knot:

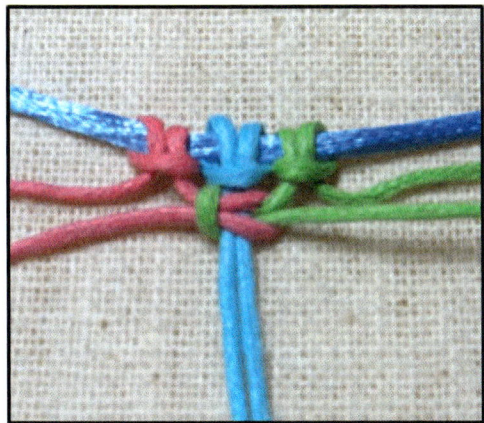

Here are several in a row, which is called a sennit.

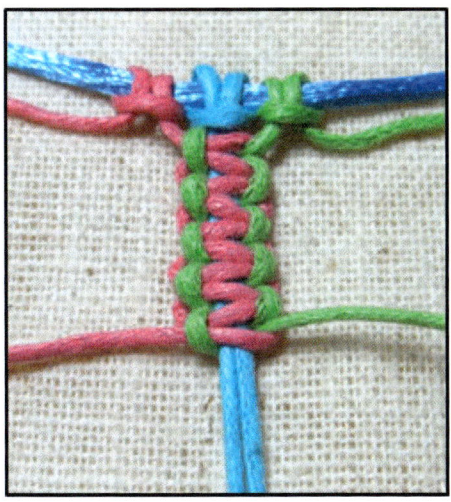

Picot Knot (aka Butterfly Knot)

Tie a regular flat knot.

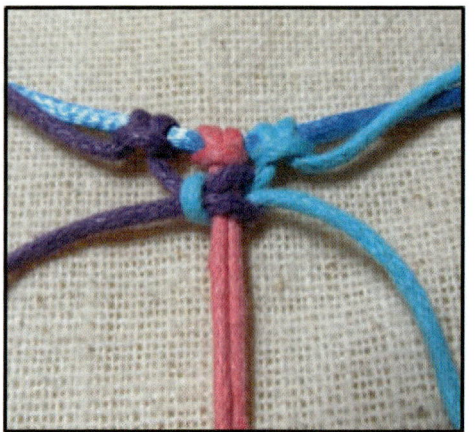

Leave a little space then tie another.

Slide this up and pull outward on the large loops in between them, until you have the desired size.

Create another flat knot.

Push it up as you gently tug to get your desired width.

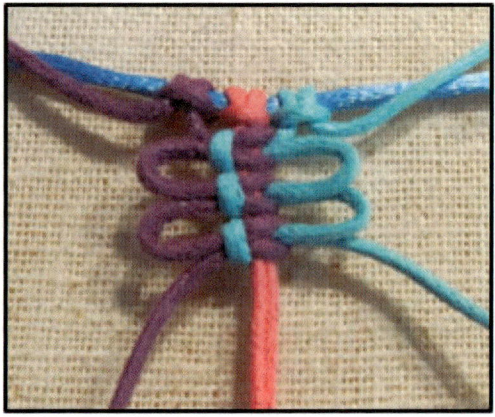

Here is a sennit of picot knots.

Spiral Knot (aka half knot)

A half knot is the first half of a flat knot (or square knot). If you tie several in a row, they naturally begin to twist and you get a spiral effect. Place the left cord over the filler cords then put the right cord over top of the left.

Slide the right cord under the filler cords then out and over the left cord.

Tighten it up. Then take the left cord again and put it over the filler cords. Lay the right cord over the left.

Thread the right cord behind the filler cords, then out and over the left cord.

Page 22

Now you can see the spiral.

Continue on, always beginning with the left hand cord and the spiral will look like this:

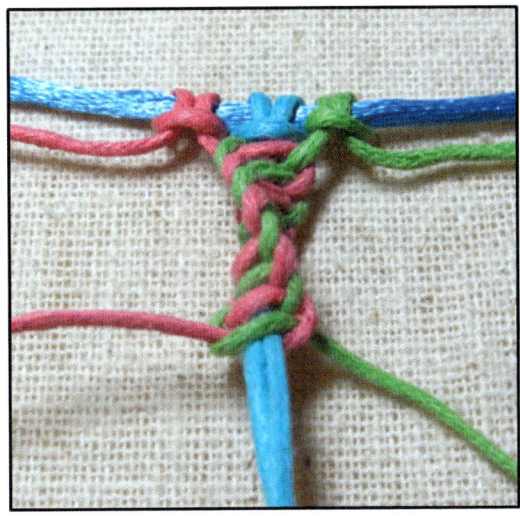

If you were to tie knots from only the right side, your spiral would twist differently and look like this:

Diagonal Double Half Hitch

This knot is a little tricky, but with just a bit of practice you should be able to get a feel for the right amount of tension and that will help you master it. You can work this knot from either side. Here we start on the left. Take the far left cord (cord 1) and lay it diagonally over top of all the other cords. Pin it in place. This is your filler or holding cord, onto which the knots will be tied.

Take the next cord in from the left – cord 2 – and from underneath wrap it up and around. Be sure the tail end of the cord passes over the cord shaft. Gently snug the knot up to the top of the holding cord.

Repeat a second time with the same cord to complete the double half hitch.

Repeat with each of the other cords. Here we are beginning the first half of the last double half hitch in this series:

Here is the second half:

This is a completed diagonal double half hitch from left to right:

Now we will work a diagonal double half-hitch from right to left. I will just continue on with the arrangement I have going. Instructions will be the same if you are starting a new project.

Take the cord from the far right and lay it diagonally over all the other cords to the left. Pin in place. This is now your holding cord. Working with the adjacent cord, wrap it up around the holding cord, making sure the tail end crosses over its own shaft.

Snug it up and repeat a second time to finish the knot.

Here is the completed piece. This is a row of DDHH from left to right, and then from right to left.

Alternating Lark's Head Knot (or chain)

This one may look harder than it is. Once you get going it is pretty easy and fun. Just think over, under, over OR under, over, under.

You can start on the left or right. Begin with the cord closest to the center holding cords, and work over, under and over as shown.

You will want to tighten that up, but for now I will show you the next half of the knot which goes under, over, under.

Page 29

Here is what it looks like cinched up:

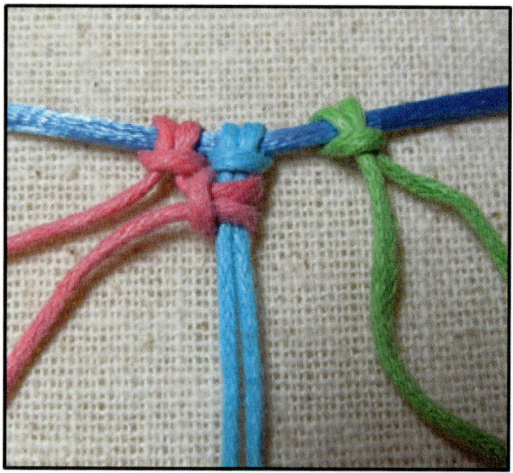

Repeat on other side with cord closest to the holding cords. Work over, under, over and draw it up tight, then work under, over, under.

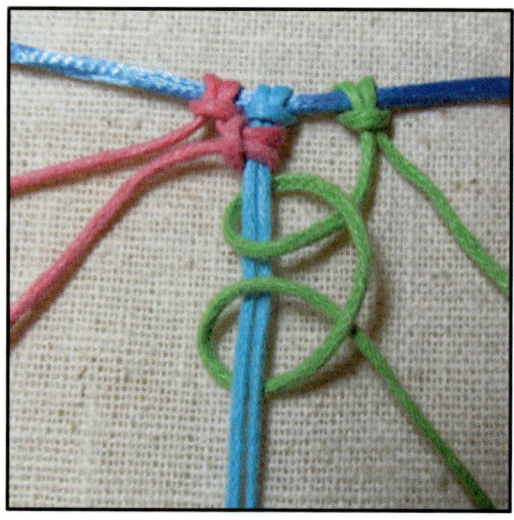

Here is the second knot finished:

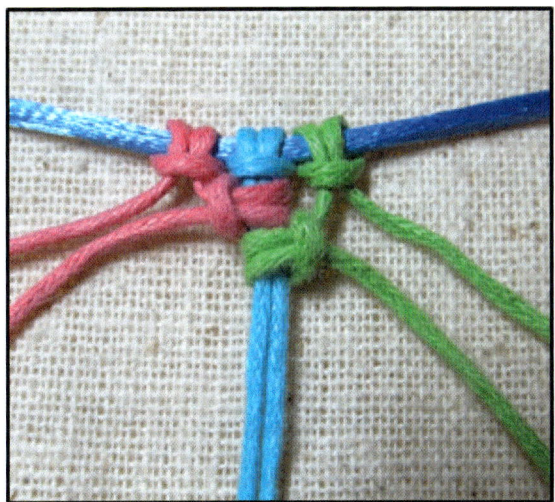

Alternate sides. I next worked with the outermost pink cord, then the outermost green cord. Here is a chain of Alternating Lark's Head knots.

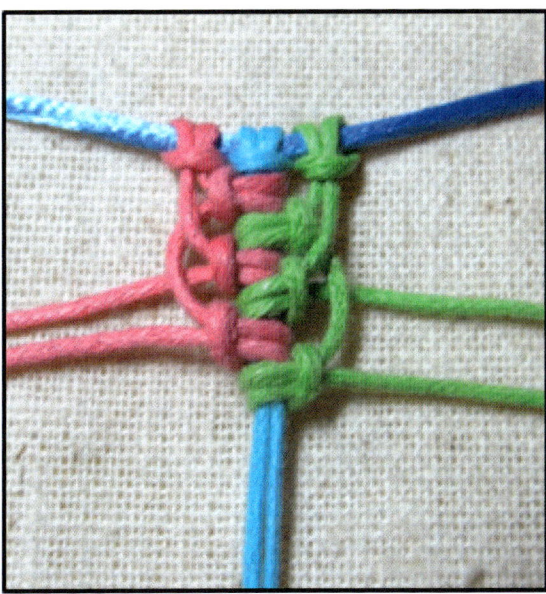

Project 1 - Summer Sunrise Earrings

Celebrating summer with another fun, original Micro Macrame design. These cheerful earrings offer a fresh look by mixing Chinese Coral C-Lon cord with pearl and iridescent beads. The cordwork section measures about 1 1/4 inches.

Knots Used:

- Lark's Head Knot
- Flat Knot (aka square knot)
- Double Half Hitch Knot

Supplies:

- C-Lon cord, 2 ft, x 10 (5 cords per earring)
- 2 antique gold jump rings
- 1 set antique gold ear wires
- 8 - 3 mm pearl beads
- 4 - 5 mm apricot beads
- 48 - size 11 iridescent peach beads
- Beacon 527 glue
- wax paper (optional)

Instructions:

Take one cord and place the ends together. Thread both through a 5 mm apricot bead, leaving a loop peeking out of the bead at one end. Place the loose ends of the cord through this open loop as shown. Attach the remaining cords, two per side using Lark's Head (LH) knots.

Tighten everything up. Now turn it upside down and pin onto your work surface, separating cords 5-5.

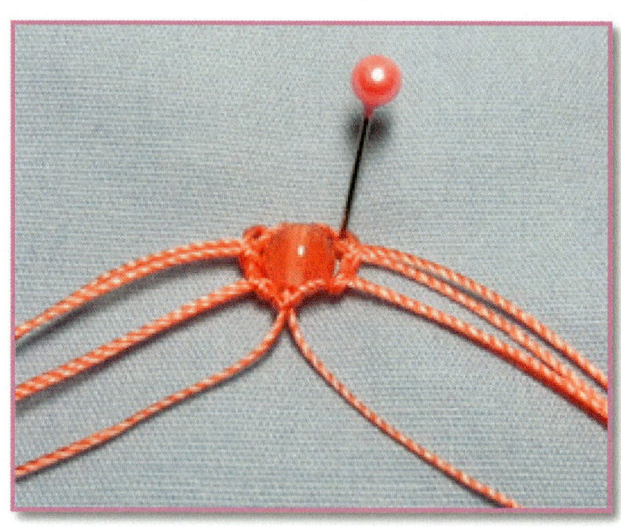

Left 5:
Gently tighten the LH knots. Find the outer left cord. Thread on a size 11 peach seed bead, then place this cord down and to the right as the Holding Cord (HC). Tie Diagonal Double Half Hitch (DDHH) knots onto it with the other 4 cords (outside to inside).

Repeat 2 more times.

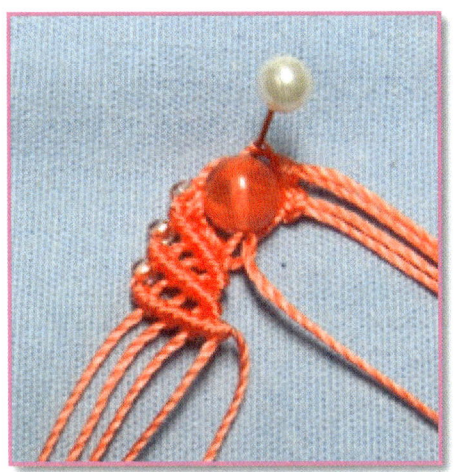

Right 5:
Tighten LH knots. Find the outer right cord. Thread on a size 11 peach seed bead, then place this cord down and to the left as the HC. Tie DDHH knots onto it with the other 4 cords (outside to inside). Repeat 2 more times.

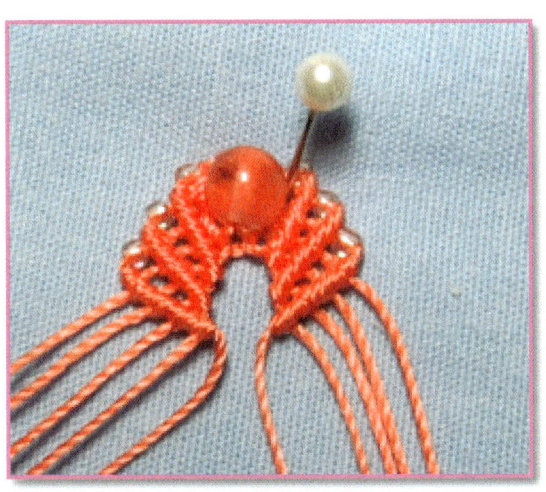

Thread a seed bead, a 3mm pearl bead and another seed bead onto each outer cord.

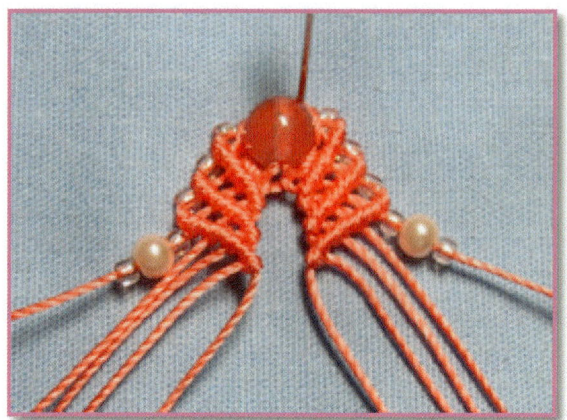

Find the center 2 cords. Place a 3mm pearl bead on each cord. Take a 5mm apricot bead and thread one cord in from each side.

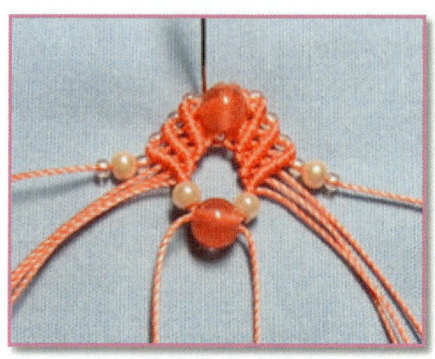

From the center, find the next cord out on the left and place on it 7 seed beads. Repeat with the next cord out (from the center) on the right.

Now use these two beaded cords to tie a flat knot around the inner 2 cords, tightening up and being mindful of bead placement.

With left 3 cords:
Using the outer left cord as the Wrapping Cord (WC), tie 10 Double Half Hitch (DHH) knots around the other 2 cords to form a bundle.

With right 3 cords:
Using the outer right cord as the WC, tie 10 DHH knots around the other 2 cords to form a bundle. Bend each of the bundles so they curve inward slightly.

Place all the cords together and tie a flat knot with the outer 2 cords, then put all the cords except the outer most on each side, through a jump ring.

Now turn it right-side up, then flip to the back. Gather all the cords that are through the jump ring and place them straight down.

Tie a flat knot with the outer 2 cords around all others.

Glue, trim, glue again. I usually sandwich the piece between layers of wax paper to avoid getting glue where I don't want it.

Place the jump ring on an earring wire, then repeat the pattern to create its mate.

Project 2 - Meandering Brook Bracelet

Combining the Margarete Lace technique with some of Micro-Macrame's most common knots creates this flowing design. Gold beads compliment the blue cord in this project, which includes a bead button closure. Finished length is 8 inches.

Knots Used:

- Overhand Knot
- Flat Knot (aka square knot)
- Alternating Lark's Head Knot
- Double Half-Hitch Knot

Supplies:

- Blue Lagoon C-lon cord 6 cords, 9 ft each
- 21 gold beads, size 6
- 21 aqua beads, size 6
- 1 aqua button bead, 7mm
- Beacon 527 glue

Instructions:

Place all 6 cords together and fold in half. Tie a loose overhand knot and pin onto your board as shown:

Using the outer most cord on each side, tie about 13 flat knots around the inner cords. Untie the overhand knot and place the flat knots in a horseshoe shape. Pin the ends in place and check to see if your button bead will fit (snugly) through the opening. Adjust flat knots as necessary.

1. Separate cords 3-3-6. With the left 3 cords; find the left cord and tie Half-hitch (HH) knots around the other 2 until you have about 2 ½ cm.

Page 43

2. With the center 3 cords: With the right cord tie an Alternating Lark's Head (ALH) knot onto the center cord. Tie an ALH knot with the left cord onto the center cord. Place a size 6 gold bead onto the center cord. Tie an ALH knot with the right cord, then the left cord. Loosen the cords around the bead just slightly to create an arc.

3. Place another gold bead onto the center cord and tie ALH knots with the right, then the left cord. Repeat once more.

4. With right 6 cords: separate 3-3. Find the outer 3 cords and tie 3 flat knots. With the inner 3 cords tie 4 flat knots.

5. Take the right cord and add on a size 6 blue bead. Put a pin next to the bead then place as the holding cord (HC) down and to the left. Tie Double Half-Hitch (DHH) knots onto it with the other 5 cords. Repeat twice more.

6. Still working with the right 6 cords: separate 3-3. Find the outer 3 cords and tie 4 flat knots this time. With the inner 3 cords tie 3 flat knots.

7. Place the left 6 cords together. Find the left cord and tie a DHH knot around the other 5, allowing the left bundle to arc outwards.

Put all 12 cords together and find the right cord. Tie a DHH knot carefully around all other cords, tightening everything up close to previous knots.

8. Separate cords 6-3-3. With the right 3 cords; find the right cord and tie a DHH knot around the other 2 until you have about 2 ½ cm.

9. Repeat step 2.
10. Repeat step 3.

11. With left 6 cords: separate 3-3. Find the outer 3 cords and tie 3 flat knots. With the inner 3 cords tie 4 flat knots.

12. Find the left cord and add on a size 6 blue bead. Place as HC down and to the right then tie DHH knots onto it with the other 5 cords. Repeat twice more.

13. With left 6 cords: separate 3-3. Find the outer 3 cords and tie 4 flat knots this time. With the inner 3 cords tie 3 flat knots.

14. Place the right 6 cords together. Find the right cord and tie a DHH knot around the other 5, allowing the right bundle to arc outwards. Place all 12 cords together and find the left cord. Tie a DHH knot carefully around all other cords, tightening everything up close to previous knots.

15. Repeat steps 1 through 7.

16. Repeat steps 8-14.

17. Repeat step 1 through 7.

Page 51

18. Repeat steps 8-14. (If you stop here the bracelet will measure about 6 ½ inches in length. Skip to step 20 to finish with a button bead closure. Otherwise continue with step 19, which will give you a finished length of about 8 inches)

19. Repeat steps 1-7.

20. Take your button bead and thread on as many cords as you can, starting with the center cords. Push the remaining cords to the back side of the bead. Carefully tie an overhand knot and tighten it up against the bead. Trim excess cords and glue well.

Project 3 - Wild Cinnamon Fern Bracelet

This micro macramé pattern uses the Margarete Lace version of knotting. Featuring a slider bead, this design is worked from the center outward. In addition to using traditional macramé knots, you will learn to wrap in bundles as you create this lovely 7 ½ inch bracelet.

Knots Used:

- Lark's Head Knot
- Double Half-Hitch Knot
- Flat Knot (aka square knot)
- Vertical Lark's Head Knot

Supplies:

- Red C-Lon cord, 4ft, x14 (7 per side)
- 1 Slider Bead (focal bead)
- Black seed beads, 34
- Gray seed beads, 32
- 1 silver 3 ring clasp closure
- 4mm black beads, 4
- Silver seed beeds, 26
- Dark grey size 6 beads, 16
- Glue - Beacon 527 mutli-use
- Silver crimp beads, I used 3mm, but you can play with it and use what works for you.

Instructions:

Place one cord through one side of the slider and center it, then tie a half-hitch knot with each end to secure it onto the slider. This is your holding cord (HC). Fold another cord in half and attach it to the HC with a Lark's Head knot (LHK). Repeat with the rest of the cords. Turn the bracelet over to the front. You now have 14 cords to work with.

Page 55

Separate 7-7.
With the left 7 cords:
Tighten the LH knots. Find the right cord. This will be our wrapping cord. Place the other 6 cords together in a bundle and tie a double half hitch (DHH) knot around them all with the wrapping cord. Tie one more DHH knot.

Now set the wrapping cord aside. Still working with this left section, find the next cord in on the right and wrap the remaining 5 cords with this one until you have about 6 DHH knots or 1 ½ cm in length.

Find the outer left cord of the bundle and set it aside. Wrap one more DHH with the same wrapping cord as before. (If the WC ends up as the leftmost cord, set it aside and pick up the next right cord as the WC).

Repeat this step until you have used all the cords. Take the bundle section and bend it out a little as shown.

Find outer left cord and thread on a silver seed bead. Slide the bead up tight and place a pin through the cord right next to the bead. Now place this cord to the right as a filler cord. Tie DHH knots onto it with the remaining cords, left to right (then set aside the holding cord). Repeat 4 times, then set aside this section.

With the right 7 cords:
Separate cords 4-3. Tighten LH knots. With the set of 4 cords; place the left cord to the right and tie DHH knots from left to right. Move the HC to the left and tie DHH knots from right to left.
Now find the 3 right cords. Use the left cord as a wrapping cord and tie 3 DHH knot around the other 2 cords.

Place the 7 right cords together. Take the right cord and put 3 black seed beads onto it. Find the second cord in from the right and place 2 black seed beads on it. The third cord in gets 1 seed bead.

Now place the cord with 1 bead on it to the left as a holding cord. Tie DHH knots with the four cords next to it, from right to left. Repeat with the next 2 cords.

Look to the left and find the top cord, the very first one you set aside. Place on it 2 gray seed beads, a 4mm black bead, followed by 2 gray seed beads.

Place these 4 cords together and lay overtop of the 6 left cords. Tie a DHH knot around all 4 cords with each of the left 6.

Working with the center 6 cords, think of them as numbered 1-6 from top to bottom and place a 3mm gray-black bead on cords 1, 3 and 5.

With the right 4 cords:
Use the inner cord as the wrapping cord and tie 4 DHH knots around the other 3 to create a bundle. Now place these 4 cords together, over top of the center 6 cords. Tie DHH knots with each of the 6 cords around the bundle.

Separate 8-6.
With the right 6 cords: place a silver seed bead on the top cord, put a pin through the cord tight against the bead, then place the cord down to the left as a HC. Tie DHH knots. Repeat with the remaining cords.

Sep 4-4-6.
Take the right 6 cords and place them under the center 4 cords. Tie a DHH knot with each of the 6 cords, around the bundle of 4 cords.

With the left 4: place 4 gray seed beads on the left cord. Skip the second cord and place 2 gray seed beads on the 3rd cord in. Use the right cord as the HC, placing it to the left. Tie DHH knots with the other 3 cords.

Now take the right cord and place it to the left as the HC. Tie DDHH knots from right to left. Slide a size 6 dark gray bead onto all 4 cords. Thread a 4mm black bead onto the center 2 cords (all 4 cords if you can) push the side cords around to the back side as you add on the next bead, which is another dark gray bead.

With the center 6 cords; place a black seed bead on the top cord, then place a pin through the cord next to the bead. Move the cord to the right and tie DHH knots onto it. Repeat with remaining center cords.

With the right 4 cords; thread on a size 6 dark gray bead. Place these cords to the left over the center 6 cords. Tie a DHH knot with each of the center cords around the bundle of 4. Wrap tight against the base of the fan.

Take one of the cords from the bundle and tie 2 more DHH knots around the bundle.

Place the 4 left cords under the center bundle. Tie DHH knots onto the bundle w/each of the left cords.

Sep cords 4-4-6.
With the left 4: place a silver seed bead on the outermost cord, pin, place to the right as HC, tie DHH knots with the other cords (set aside HC as before) Repeat until you have used all of the 4 left cords.

With the right 6 cords; Place right cord to the left tight against previous row and tie DHH knots from right to left. Skip the outer 2 cords, put the next 2 cords together and thread on a size 6 dark gray bd. On the outer cord place a black seed bead, then use this cord to tie a vertical LH knot onto the cord next to it. Repeat twice more.

Move the HC from the left to the right and tie DHH knots from the inside out. Now place the HC to the left and tie DHH knots from the outside in. Repeat above beading sequence and DHH knots from left to right.

Center 4: tie a flat knot around the center 2 cords, thread outer cords (back to front) through the cord openings on the DHH knots on the left & right. Now bead the center 2 cords with gray seed beads; 3 each.

Tie another flat knot.

Sep cords 8-6.
Left 8: find the outer cord on each side and tie 2 flat knots.
Tie 1 flat knot w/right 6 cords.

Place all cords together and tie a flat knot with the outer most cords.

Sep cords 4-3-3-4. Crimp beads; you can use large crimp beads (3mm) with the sets of 4 cords. Smaller crimp beads will work for the center sets of 3 cords, if you have them. Both sets of 3 go through the inner loop of the clasp. Crimp, turn over, glue, trim. (another closure option is shown on the next page)

Another option is to use a large crimp bead and an adjustable necklace clasp as shown here.

Whichever you prefer, repeat for second side of the bracelet.

Other color scheme examples:

Project 4 - Island Cove Necklace

Create a pendant! Beaded cord is attached to your finished micro-macrame centerpiece. Tropical lagoon colors combine to create the ebb and flow of this project. Anchoring things together is a lobster clasp. The finished length, stem to stern, is 10 inches. Cast off your cares and enjoy smooth sailing with this design!

Knots Used:

- Verticle Lark's Head Knot
- Flat Knot (aka square knot)
- Half-Hitch Knot

Supplies:

- Blush C-Lon cord, 6 ft cord (x4), 2 1/2 ft cord (x1), 1 ft cord (x2)
- 12mm Teal beads (x5)
- 8mm Tan beads (x8)
- Size 11 seed beads, teal (x14)
- 2.5mm Gold Crimp beads (x2)
- Size 6 seed beads, assorted teal and bronze (x133)
- 2mm Gold crimp beads (x2)
- Antique gold leaves, about 1mm (x3)
- Gold lobster clasp and jump ring
- Large gold crimp bead (U-shaped, might be labled for leather cord) (x2)
- Glue - Beacon 527 mutli-use

Instructions:

1. Place 4 cords through the ring at the top of an end crimp clasp. Fold the cords in half, for a total of 8 cords. Lay the cords in the crimp; glue and crimp shut. Turn over.

Tie a flat knot with outer 2 cords around all others.

2. Separate 3-3-2.
With the left 3: Find the left cord and tie 7 Vertical Lark's Head (VLH) knots around the other 2 cords.

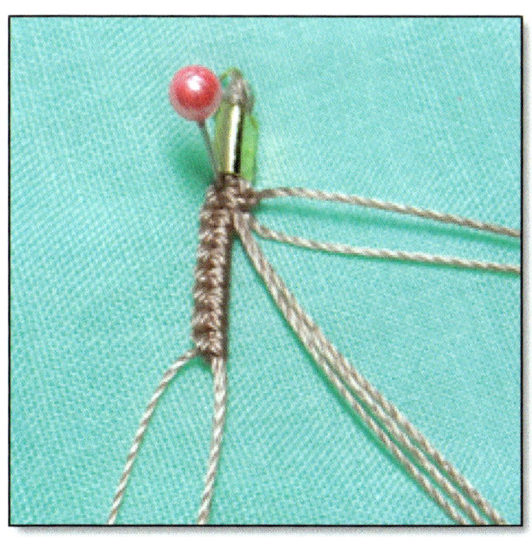

3. With the center 3: Find the left cord and tie 3 VLH knots around the other 2 cords.

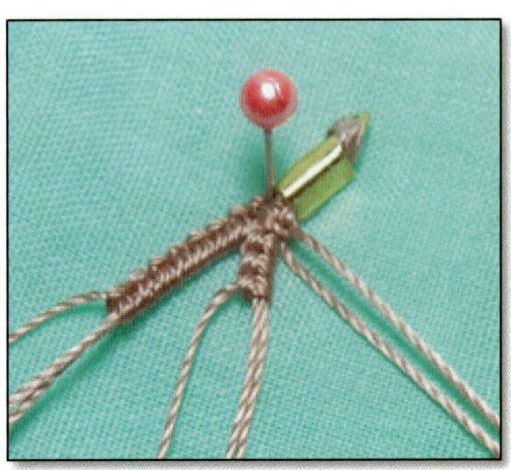

4. Place all 6 cords together. Bend the left section outwards, then take the left cord and tie a VLH knot around the other 5 cords. NOTE: tighten up each section as you attach them together.

5. With the left 3: Find the left cord and tie 5 VLH knots around the other 2 cords.

6. With the center 3: Thread a size 6 teal bead onto all 3 cords.

7. Place the left 6 cords together. Arc the left section outwards, then take the left cord and tie a VLH knot around the other 5 cords. (NOTE: tighten up each section as you attach them together).

8. With the left 3: Find the left cord and tie 7 VLH knots around the other 2 cords.

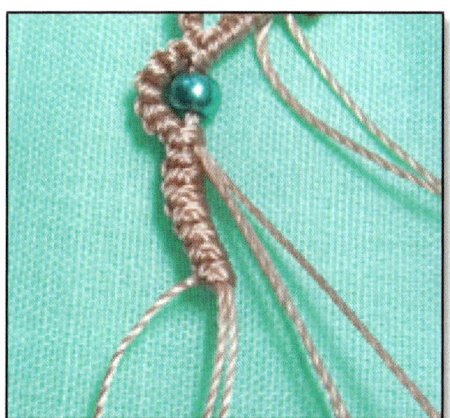

9. With the center 3: Find the left cord and tie 3 VLH knots around the other 2 cords.

10. Place these 6 cords together. Arc the left section outwards, then take the left cord and tie a VLH knot around the other 5 cords. (Remember to tighten things up). Set aside this section.

11. Using the right 2 cords: With the outer cord, tie 3 VLH knots onto the inner cord, then place a seed bead onto the outer cord. Tie 2 VLH knots, then place a seed bead onto the outer cord. Tie 2 VLH knots with the outer cord, then put a seed bead onto the outer cord and tie 3 VLH knots.

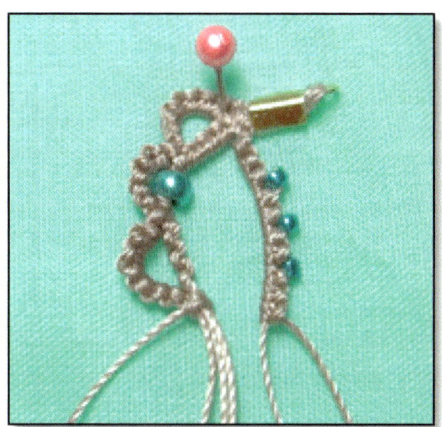

Place all 8 cords together and find the left cord. Use it to tie a VLH knot around all others.

12. Repeat steps 2 to 11 to create the second section. Note: when starting the second section, move one of the longer cords to the outside to use as the knotting cord. You won't be able to tell that you snuck it over there.

Center Section

13. Separate cords 2-2-3-1. Find the right cord and thread on a bronze size 6 bead, a 12mm teal bead and another bronze size 6 bead. Set aside.

14. Find the right 3 cords. Using the right cord as the wrapping cord (WC), tie half hitch (HH) knots to create a bundle 3 ½ cm long. Set aside.

15. With the center 2 cords: Move the longest cord to the left and use as the WC. Tie 9 VLH knots.

16. With left 2: Move the longer cord to the left to use as the WC. Tie 13 VLH knots.

17. Put the 4 left cords together and tie a VLH knot with the left cord. Place 3 size 6 beads on the right 2 cords (teal, gold, teal).

18. With the left 2: Tie 8 VLH knots. Put the 4 cords together and tie a VLH knot with the left cord.

19. With left 2, tie 13 VLH knots. With right 2, tie 9 VLH knots. Place the 4 cords together and tie a VLH knot with the left cord.

Put all 8 cords together and tie a VLH knot with the left cord. (End of Center Section)

20. Repeat steps 2 through 11 twice. Note: tighten up the right 2 cords before working with them. If you start with the right cords here it will lock things in place.

Turn the piece over and place the cords in the large crimp bead. Glue in place and crimp shut. Trim the ends.

Finishing

1. Place together the 2 ½ ft cord and one of the 1 ft cords, keeping the longer cord on the right. Thread them through the 2.5mm crimp bead, the lobster clasp and back through the crimp bead. Crimp the crimp bead.

2. Bead as follows: (Note: when beading be careful to keep the longer cord on the right at all times. If the cords get twisted inside the beads, it will skew the design).

3. Onto both cords; 1 dark teal, 1 frosted teal, 1 teal, 1 light copper, 1 dark copper, 1 light copper, 1 teal, 1 frosted teal, 1 dark teal followed by an 8mm tan bead. Repeat 3 times.

4. Place on both cords 1 dark teal, 1 frosted teal, 1 teal, 1 light copper, 1 dark copper and 1 light copper. Now separate the cords, with the longest cord to the right.

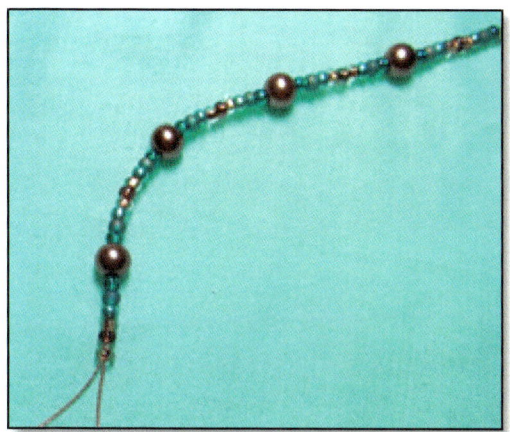

5. Onto the left cord only place 1 teal, 1 frosted teal, 1 dark teal, 1 light copper, 1 dark copper, 1 light copper, then 1 dark teal, 1 frosted teal and 1 teal. Now attach this cord to the pendant with a 2mm crimp bead.

6. Onto the right cord place: 1 dark teal, 1 gold, 1 bronze bead. Then the 12mm teal bead followed by a gold, 2 frosted teal and another gold bead. Thread on a 12mm teal, then a bronze, 2 dark teal and another bronze bead.

7. Put on a gold leaf, a size 11 teal seed bead and repeat that once more then follow up with a third gold leaf.

8. Continue beading with a bronze, 2 dark teal and another bronze bead followed by the 12mm teal bead. A size 6 gold, 2 frosted teal and another gold bead go on next, then the last 12mm teal bead. Now 1 bronze, 1 gold, and 1 dark teal.

9. Tighten up the beading. Take the remaining 1 ft cord and attach it to the right side of the pendant with a 2mm crimp bead.

10. Continue beading as shown – matching the first side (remember to keep the cords parallel inside the beads).

11. Thread both cords through the 2.5mm crimp bead then through the jump ring and back through the crimp bead.

12. Tighten up the beading then crimp the crimp bead. Glue and trim.

Project 5 - Lacey Sea Coral Bracelet

Fashion this striking bracelet by utilizing 2 colors of c-lon cord and several knots, including the Margarete Lace bundling technique. This dainty piece has a button closure and is about 7 inches in wearable length (to the beginning of button closure) to lengthen; add flat knots before threading on the button bead.

Knots Used:

- Overhand Knot
- Double Half Hitch Knot
- Flat Knot (aka square knot)
- Vertical Lark's Head Knot

Supplies:

- Apricot C-Lon cord, 8 ft (x3)
- Ginger C-Lon cord, 8 ft (x3)
- 1 peach button bead (mine is 8mm with a center large enough to fit onto 8 cords)
- 4 peach 5mm beads (must fit onto 2 cords)
- 96 peach seed beads (size 11) OR 48 size 6 beads; peach (I couldn't find any size 6 beads the right size and color, so I bought the seed beads and used 2 at a time)
- Glue - Beacon 527 mutli-use

Instructions:

1. Place all 6 cords together and find the center (color placement does not matter for this pattern. The colors fall where they may throughout. Feel free to use 1 color if you like). Tie a loose overhand knot at the center point and place the cords on your project board as shown:

2. Using the outer most cord on each side, tie about 12 flat knots around the inner 4 cords. Untie the overhand knot and place the flat knots in a horse-shoe shape. Pin the ends in place and check to see if your button bead will fit (snugly) through the opening. Adjust flat knots as necessary.

Find the outer 2 cords and tie 2 flat knots around all other cords.

3. Shell section: Find the right cord (called the wrapping cord or WC) and tie a double half-hitch (DHH) around all other cords.

Set aside this right cord. Find the outer left cord and tie another DHH knot around all other cords. Repeat this step, alternating right and left cords until you have used them all. You now have 6 cords on the right and 5 on the left, so move the remaining cord to the left.

Place 2 size 11 seed beads (or 1 size 6 bead) on the top right cord. Find the bottom cord and place it up to the right, against the bead, as the holding cord (HC). Tie DHH knots onto the HC, from bottom to top.

Place 2 seed beads (or 1 size 6 bead) on the top left cord. Find the bottom cord and place it up to the left, against the bead, as the HC. Tie DHH knots onto the HC, from bottom to top.

Working w/the right cords:
Thread 2 size 11 seed beads (or 1 size 6) onto the top right cord, put a pin right next to the beads, then place the cord down and in toward the center, as the HC. Tie DHH knots onto the HC working from the top to the bottom. Set HC aside and repeat with each cord until you have used them all.

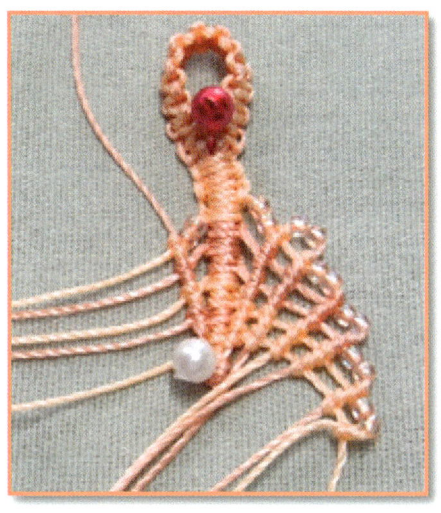

Working w/the left cords:
Thread 2 seed beads onto the top left cord, put a pin right next to the beads, then place the cord down and in toward the center, as the HC. Tie DHH knots onto the HC working from the top to the bottom. Set the HC aside and repeat with each cord until you have used them all.

4. Loop Section: Separate cords 6-6. On the left; place a pin in your board at the end NEXT TO the last, smallest DHH knot, to hold a place open. Find this last HC, place it up to the right (around the shaft of the pin) and pin in place.

Take the cord on the left and tie a DHH knot onto the HC, leaving a space by the pin. Then place this tying cord with the HC. Find the next left cord and tie a DHH knot onto both HC's, working tight against previous shell shape. Repeat with all left cords, creating a bundle.

Place the bundled cords straight out to the right. Take the lowest cord and tie a DHH knot around the bundle. Move the bundle down a bit and tie another DHH knot. Move cords straight down. Find the right cord (in the bundle) and tie the first half of a DHH knot (a half hitch), then place a pin next to the cords (on the right side) and tie the second half. The pin will hold a place open.

Set aside the cord on the right. Find the left cord and tie a DHH knot with it, then set aside a cord on the right. Repeat until you have used them all.

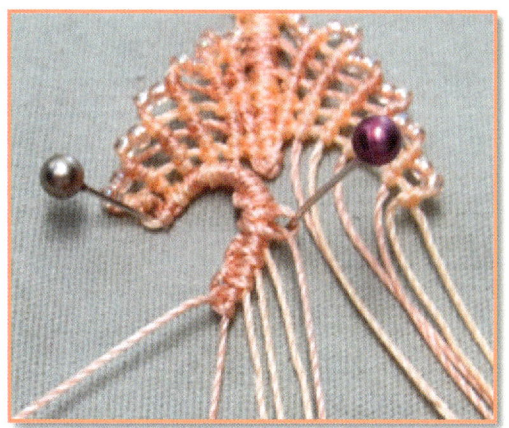

Take the last WC and thread through the opening at the end of the shell shape; front to back (use a needle if necessary). Tie a DHH knot around the HC (with the WC).

On the right; place a pin in your board at the end NEXT TO the last, smallest DHH knot, holding a place open. Find this last HC, place it up to the left (around the shaft of the pin) and pin in place.

Take the cord on the right and tie a DHH knot onto the HC, leaving a space by the pin. Then place this tying cord with the HC. Find the next right cord and tie a DHH knot onto both HC's, working tight against previous shell shape. Repeat until you have used all the cords.

Place bundled cords to the left. Take the lowest cord and tie a DHH knot around the bundle. Move the bundle down a bit and tie another DHH knot.

Move cords straight down.

Find the left cord and tie the first half of a DHH knot (a half hitch), then place this wrapping cord through the opening held open by the pin on the left set of cords. Tie the second half of the DHH knot.

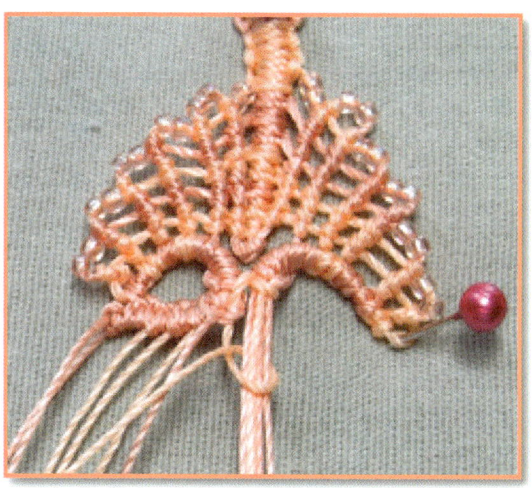

Set aside the cord on the left. Find the right cord and tie a DHH knot with it, then set aside a cord on the left. Repeat until you have used them all. Take the last WC and thread through the opening at the end of the shell shape (front to back), then tie a DHH knot around the HC.

5. Large Bead Section: Separate 2-2-4-2-2. Find outer left cord and tie 7 Vertical Lark's Head (VLH) knots onto the cord next to it. Set aside. Find the next 2 cords and tie 5 VLH knots (outer cord onto inner cord). Set aside. Repeat with the right cords.

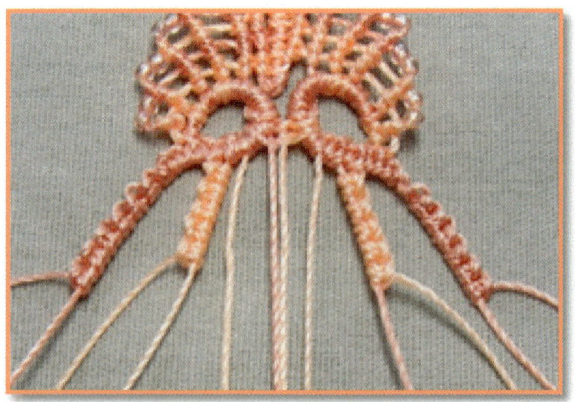

Tie a flat knot with the center 4 cords (first tightening previous knots, if necessary), then place a 5mm bead onto all 4 cords, followed by another flat knot.

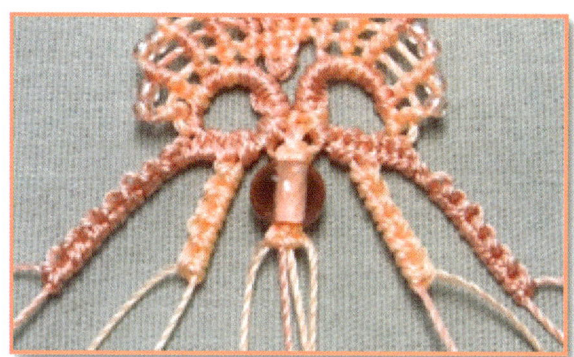

Place center 4 cords together and add to them the HC from the VLH knots sequence on each side of it. Take the next cord on each side and tie a flat knot around the bundle, snug up against previous flat knot.

Add the HC from each side to the bundle, then tie a flat knot with the remaining outer cords.

6. Repeat Shell section.

7. Repeat Loop section.

8. Repeat Large Bead section.

9. Repeat Shell section.

10. Repeat Loop section.

11. Repeat Large Bead section.

12. Repeat Shell section.

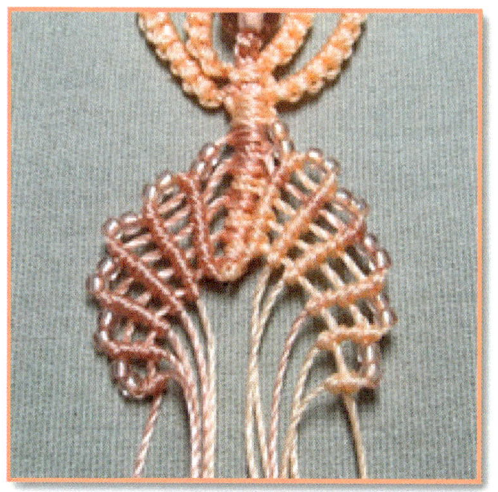

Page 101

13. Repeat Loop section.

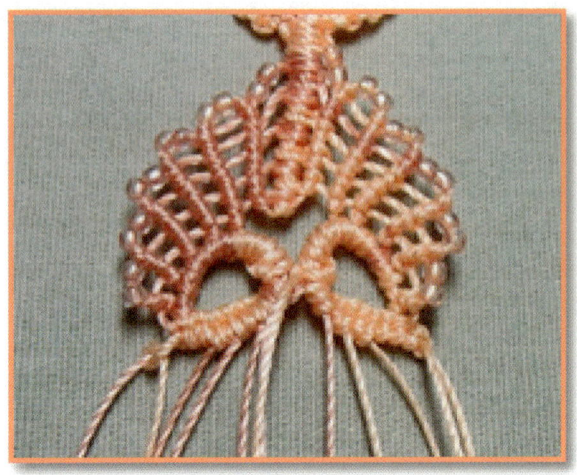

14. Repeat Large Bead section.

15. You now have 4 complete sections. Tie 1 more flat knot. Beginning with the center cords, put as many cords as you can through your button bead (I have 8 cords through mine). Tie a flat knot (I used both cords on each side as tying cords). Tie an overhand knot. Tighten, glue, and trim excess cords. Done!

Project 6 - Pizzaz Anklet

This pattern seemed to write itself as an uncomplicated, fun piece. The use of multiple cord colors keeps it cheery while offering many design choices. For ease of use it has a button closure. The pattern creates a 10 inch anklet… just repeat the pattern to enlarge, but remember to cut your cord a bit longer than specified.

Knots Used:

- Vertical Lark's Head Knot
- Flat Knot (aka square knot)
- Double Double Half Hitch Knot

Supplies:

- C-Lon cord, 5 ft 6 in., Rose (x1), Mint (x1), Apricot (x1)
- 5mm button bead (x1)
- Light green size 11 seed beads (x108)
- Pink size 11 seed beads (x64)
- Light pink size 6 seed beads (x40)
- Beacon 527 glue

Instructions:

1. Place all 3 cords together and find the center. Tie a loose overhand knot at the center point and place the cords on your project board as shown with the green on the left and the pink on the right:

Page 105

2. Using the outer most cord on each side, tie about 10 flat knots around the inner cords. Untie the overhand knot and place the flat knots in a horseshoe shape. Pin the ends in place and check to see if your button bead will fit (snugly) through the opening. Adjust flat knots as necessary.

3. Rearrange the cords so that both green cords are on the left, the apricot cords are in the center and both pink cords are on the right. Using the outer cord on each side (green and a pink) tie a flat knot.

Page 106

4. Separate the cords 2-2-2. Find the second cord in from each side and thread on 3 size 11 light green seed beads.

5. Take the left apricot cord and tie a VLH knot onto the beaded cord to the left of it. Tug gently on the apricot cord to form an arc. Now take the right apricot cord and thread it through the arc, then tie a VLH knot onto the beaded cord to the right. Tug gently on the apricot cord to form an arc.

6. Find the left cord (green) and attach it to the beaded green cord with a VLH knot. Tug gently to create an arc to the outside. Repeat with the right cord (pink onto pink).

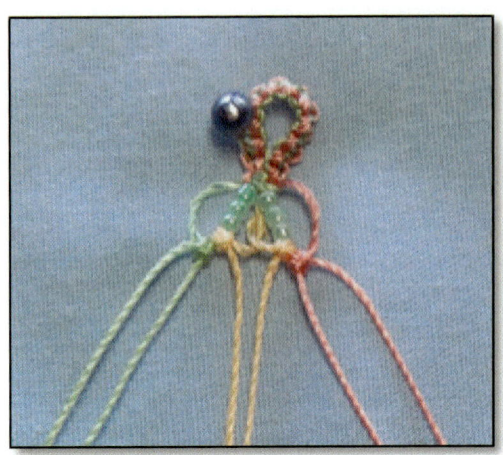

7. Repeat steps 4-6, then tie a flat knot with the outer cord on each side. Note: As you go on, if the left green cord is getting too short, swap it with the longer green cord next to it either before or after this flat knot.

8. Take the left cord and thread on four size 11 pink seed beads, one size 6 pale pink seed bead and another four size 11 pink seed beads, then set it aside. Find the right cord (pink) and place it to the left, over the other 4 cords, as the holding cord (HC). Tie diagonal double half hitch (DDHH) knots onto it from right to left.

9. Find the right cord and thread onto it three pale pink size 6 beads. Skip the next cord in and place on the next cord a size 6 pale pink bead.

Page 109

10. Take the HC from the left and place it to the right. Tie DDHH knots onto it from left to right. Retrieve the set aside cord and use it along with the far right cord to tie a flat knot around the other cords.

Repeat steps 4 through 10 until you have reached 9 1/2 inches. With the center 2 cords, thread 2 or 4 cords through the button bead. Use the remaining cords to tie a flat knot around it. Glue the back of the flat knot and let dry. Then trim the cords and glue once more.

For this one I used Teal, Blue Lagoon and Amethyst cord:

Project 7 - Micro Macrame Cross

Some people think that a cross is a horrendous thing and as such should not be beautified. Even though the cross itself is an ancient instrument of death, I view His sacrifice on the cross as a magnificent gift to be honored.

This versatile piece may be used as a Christmas tree ornament, rear view mirror décor, a bookmark, gift box decoration or to be add onto a bible cover. The large cross measures about 5 ¾ inches by 4 ¼ inches, while the smaller one is about 4 ¼ inches by 3 ¼ inches.

Knots Used:

- Vertical Lark's Head Knot
- Flat Knot (aka square knot)
- Diagonal Double Half Hitch Knot
- Butterfly Knot
- Lark's Head Knot

Supplies:

- White C-Lon cord, 3 ft 5 in. (x15) AND 4 ft cord (x5)
- 4mm or 5mm Iridescent Bicone beads (x10)
- Silver jump ring
- Beacon 527 glue

Instructions:

1. Take one of the 3 ft 5 in cords and fold it in half. Place it on your work surface sideways:

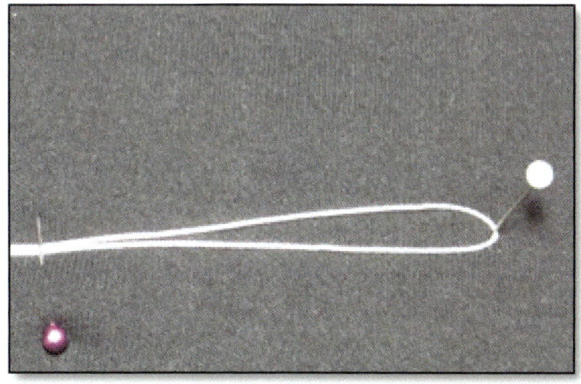

Attach the rest of the short cords by tying them onto both cords via a Lark's Head Knot (LHK).

Now add the long cords, also using the LHK.

2. Take the loose ends of the original cord and thread them through the open loop. Pull gently until you have a circle, then tighten up the cords. (The two cords you pull through join the short cords next to them). If you like, you can mark the longer cords at this point by tying them with some yarn, or marking them with tape.

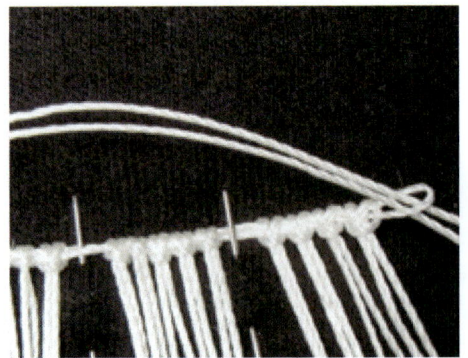 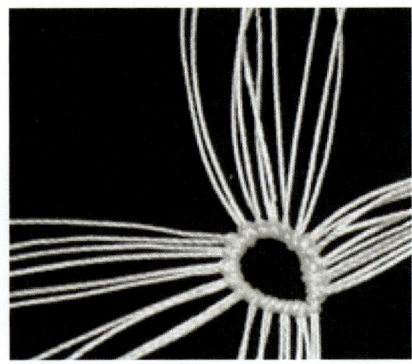

3. Find the 2 outermost cords of each section and place them together in the diagonal spaces.

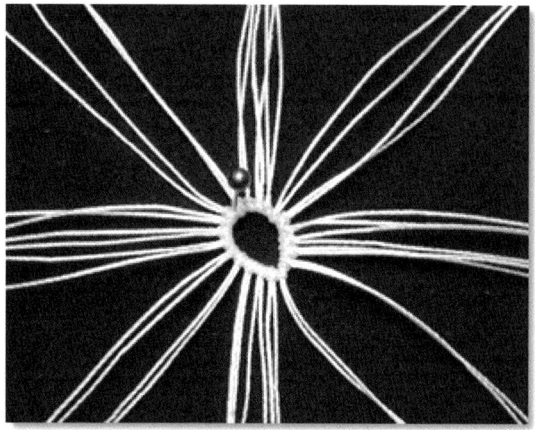

With each diagonal section tie a flat knot followed by a butterfly knot. Then return the diagonal cords to their original places (2 to each section).

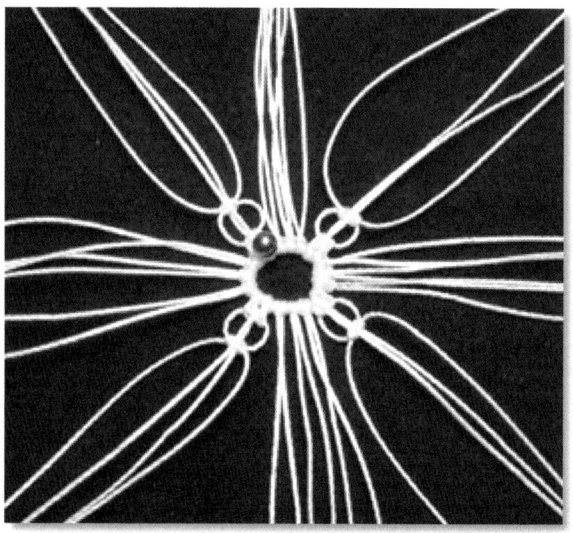

4. Working with one section of 10 cords; separate cords 5-5. Find the center cords and place each down and out as the Holding Cord (HC). At this point I recommend pinning the butterfly knots in place. Tie Diagonal Double Half Hitch (DDHH) knots onto each HC from the center out. Leave the outer cord aside. Find the inner 8 cords and tie a flat knot around the inner 6 cords. Repeat for each of the other 3 sections.

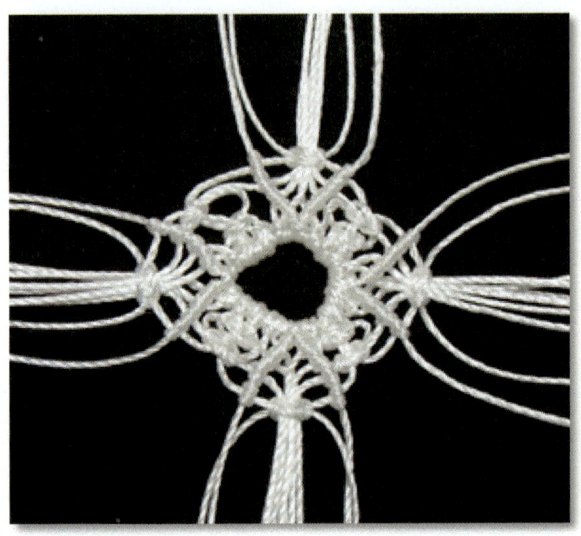

5. Go back to your original set of short cords. Tighten up the flat knot then find the outer cords and place them down and in. Tie DDHH knots onto them to complete the diamond shape. Place the right HC over the left HC. Tie a DHHK onto the right HC with the left to close the diamond.

6. Separate cords 2-2-2-2-2. With both outer sets of 2: Use the outside cord and tie 5 Vertical Lark's Head (VLH) knots onto the inner cord.

With the next set of 2 in (for each side) tie 3 VLH knots with the outer cord onto the inner cord. Note: Anytime your Wrapping Cord (WC) is getting short, you can move the longer cord over to tie VLHK with.

7. Place the center 2 cords through a 4 or 5 mm iridescent bead. Separate the cord 4-2-4. With the left 4, use the outer cord to tie a VLH knot onto the other 3. Repeat with the right 4 cords.

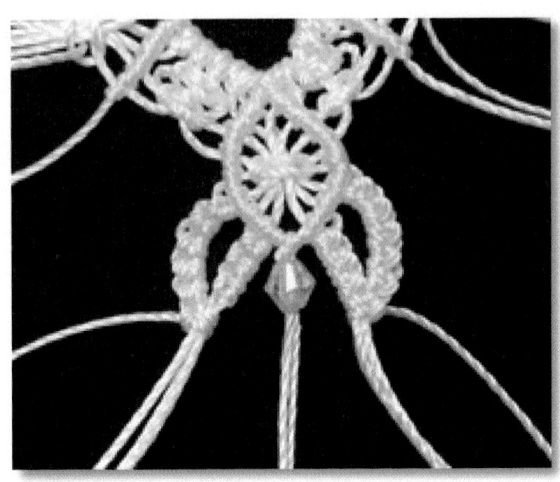

8. Separate cords 5-5. Find the inner cord on the right and place it down and to the left. Find the inner left cord (the one that is beaded) and use it to tie a DDHH knot onto the cord you just moved to the left. This will secure the top of the diamond shape. Now place the HC to the left and the WC to the right. Tie DDHH knots onto each HC from the inside to the outside.

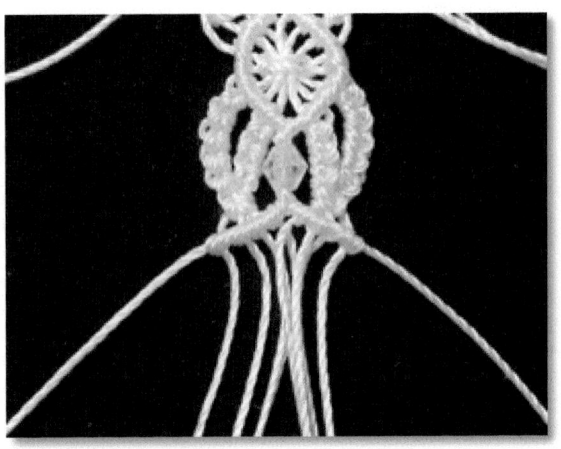

Set aside both HC's. With the outer cord on each side, tie a flat knot around the other 6 cords.

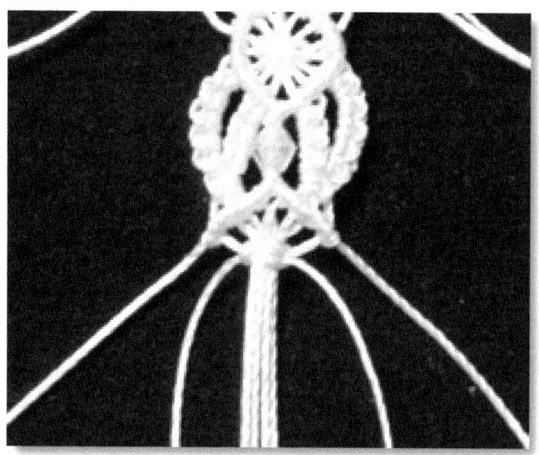

9. Separate 5-5. Move the holding cords down and in and tie DDHH knots to complete the diamond. Place right HC to the left and tie a DDHH knot with the left HC to close.

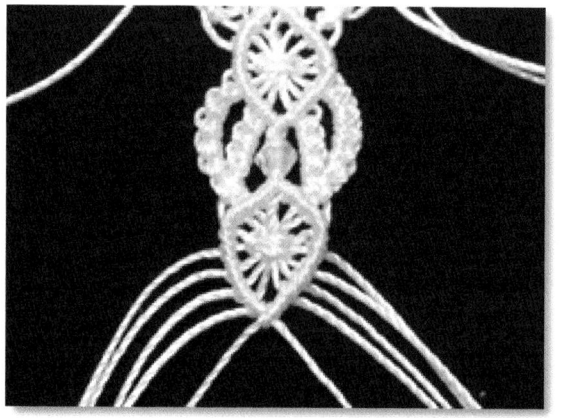

10. Find the left cord and place it down and in as the HC. Put a pin in the HC near the top. Tie DDHH knots from the outside in.

Repeat on the right side.

Place the left HC under the right and tie one more DDHH knot to close.

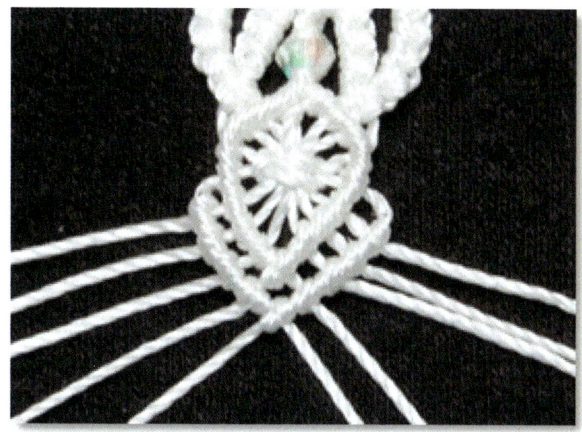

11. Separate 3-4-3. With each set of 3, tie 7 VLH knots with the outer cord onto the other 2. Find the center 4 cords and tie a flat knot, then thread on a 4 or 5mm iridescent bead. Tie a butterfly knot followed by another flat knot.

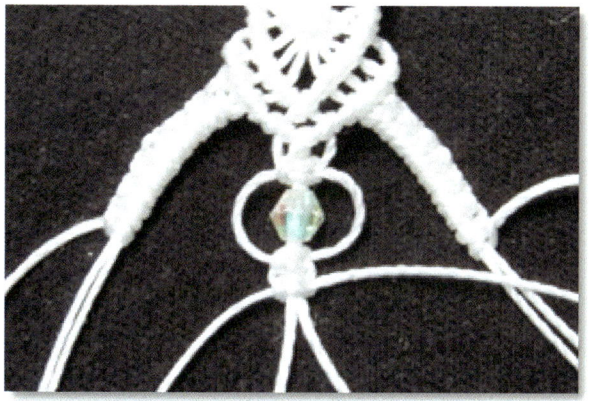

12. Separate 5-5. Take the outer cord on each side and tie a VLH knot around the other 4 cords.

Now put all the cords together and tie a flat knot with the outer 2 cords, bending the VLHK sections to form an arc.

13. Repeat steps 5 - 12 for the other 2 short sections.

Working with the long section:
14. Repeat steps 5 through 9.
15. Repeat steps 6 through 9 twice, which gives you four complete diamonds.

Now repeat steps 10 through 12.

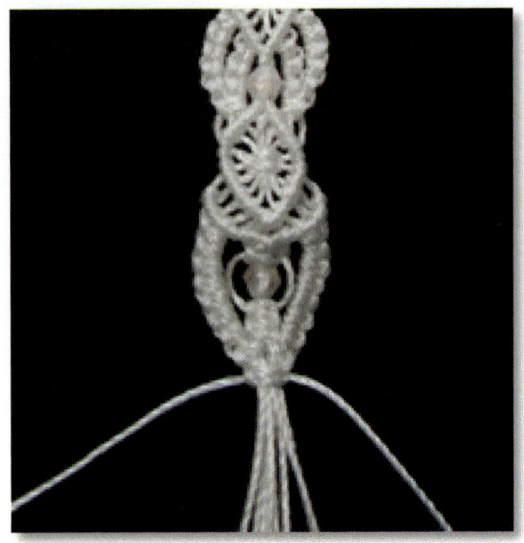

17. Place the cross right-side up, then flip it over. Put the 8 center cords through a jump ring. Bring these cords straight down, then tie a flat knot with the two outer cords.

Glue, trim, and glue again.

Small Cross

Knots Used:

- Vertical Lark's Head Knot
- Flat Knot (aka square knot)
- Diagonal Double Half Hitch Knot
- Butterfly Knot
- Lark's Head Knot

Supplies:

- White C-Lon cord, 2 ft (x15) AND 2 ft 8in cord (x5)
- 4mm or 5mm Iridescent Bicone beads (x5)
- Silver jump ring
- Beacon 527 glue

Instructions:

1. Fold one short cord in half and place horizontally on your board. Attach all remaining short cords to it, via a Lark's Head Knot (LHK).

Now attach the longer cords, also using a LHK.

2. Take the loose ends of the original cord and thread them through the open loop. Pull gently until you have a circle, then tighten up the cords. (The two cords you pull through join the short cords next to them). If you like, you can mark the longer cords at this point by tying them with some yarn, or marking them with tape.

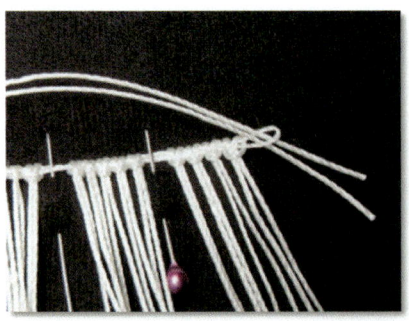 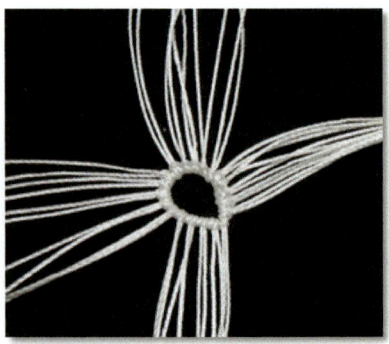

3. Find the 2 outermost cords of each section and place them together in the diagonal spaces.

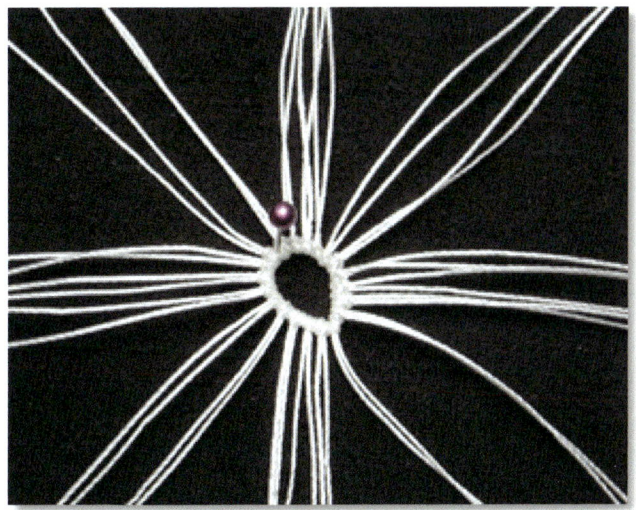

With each diagonal section tie a flat knot followed by a butterfly knot.

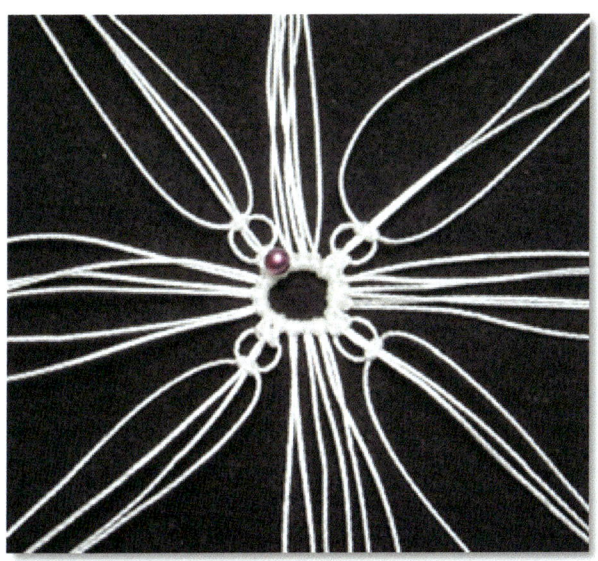

Return the diagonal cords to their original places (2 to each section).

4. Working with one section of 10 short cords; separate cords 5-5. Find the center cords and place each down and out as the Holding Cord (HC). At this point I recommend pinning the butterfly knots in place. Now tie Diagonal Double Half Hitch (DDHH) knots onto each HC from the center out. Leave the outer cord aside. Find the inner 8 cords and tie a flat knot around the inner 6 cords. Repeat for each of the other 3 sections.

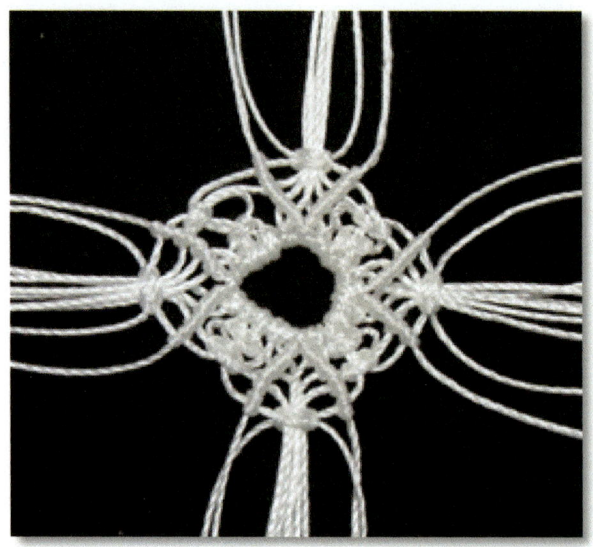

5. Go back to your original set of short cords. Tighten up the flat knot then find the outer cords and place them down and in. Tie DDHH knots onto them to complete the diamond shape. Place the right HC over the left HC. Tie a DHH knot onto the right HC with the left to close the diamond.

6. Find the left cord and place it down and in as the HC. Put a pin in the HC near the top. Tie DDHH knots from the outside in.

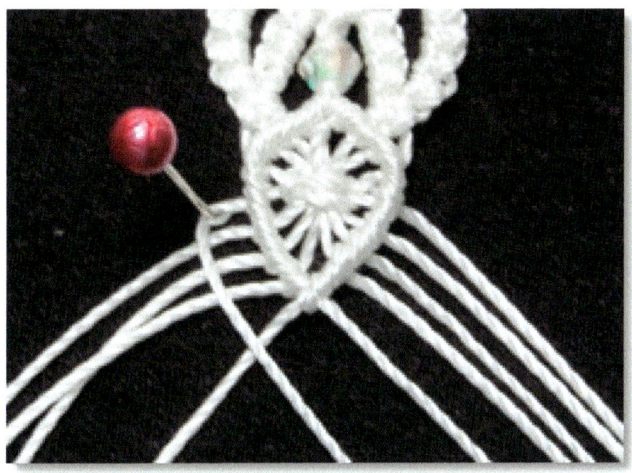

Repeat on the right side.

Place the right HC over the left HC and tie another DDHH knot with the left to close the diamond.

7. Separate cords 3-4-3. With each set of 3, tie 7 Vertical Lark's Head (VLH) knots with the outer cord onto the other 2. Find the center 4 cords and tie a flat knot then thread on a 4 or 5mm iridescent bead. Tie a butterfly knot followed by another flat knot.

8. Separate 5-5. Take the outer cord on each side and tie a VLH knot around the other 4 cords.

Now put all the cords together and tie a flat knot with the outer 2 cords, bending the VLH knot sections to form an arc.

9. Repeat steps 5 through 8 for each short section.

Working with the long section:
10. Repeat step 5.

11. Separate cords 2-2-2-2-2. With both outer sets of 2: Use the outside cord and tie 5 VLH knots onto the inner cord. With the next set of 2 in (for each side) tie 3 VLH knots with the outer cord onto the inner cord. Note: Anytime your WC is getting short, you can move the longer cord over to tie VLHK with.

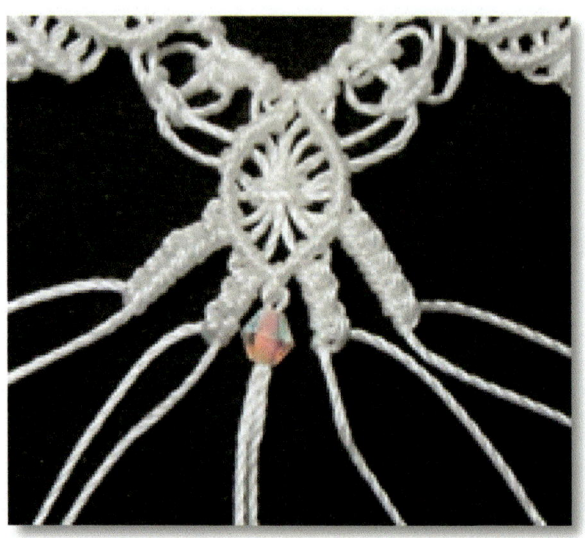

12. Place the center 2 cords through a 4 or 5 mm iridescent bead. Separate cords 4-2-4. With the left 4, find the outer cord and tie a VLH knot onto the other 3. Repeat with the right 4 cords.

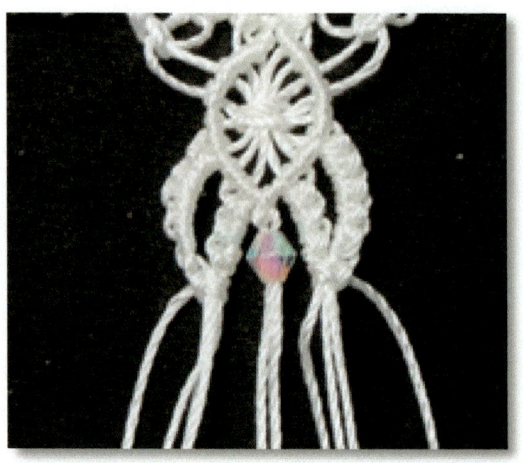

13. Separate cords 5-5. Find the inner cord on the right and place it down and to the left. Find the inner left cord (the one that is beaded) and use it to tie a DDHH knot onto the cord you just moved to the left. This will secure the top of the diamond shape. Set aside both HC's. With the outer cord on each side, tie a flat knot around the other 6 cords.

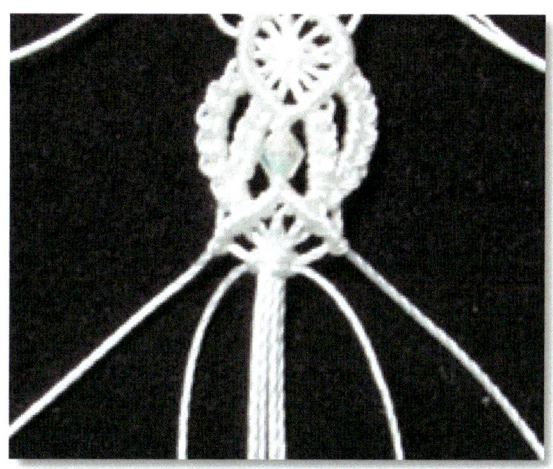

14. Separate 5-5. Move the holding cords down and in and tie DDHH knots to complete the diamond. Place the right HC to the left and tie a DDHH knot with the left HC to close the diamond.

15. Find the left cord and place it down and in as the HC. Put a pin in the HC near the top. Tie DDHH knots from the outside in. Repeat on the right side. Place the left HC under the right and tie one more DDHH knot to close.

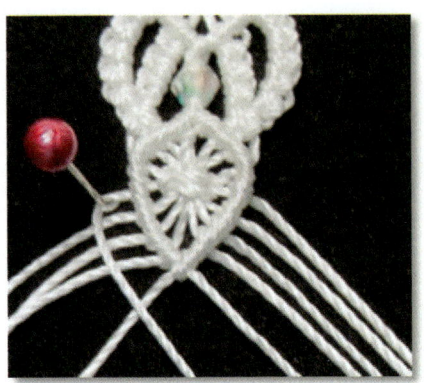 

16. Separate cords 3-4-3. With each set of 3, tie 7 VLH knots with the outer cord onto the other 2. Find the center 4 cords and tie a flat knot, then thread on a 4 or 5mm iridescent bead. Tie a butterfly knot followed by another flat knot.

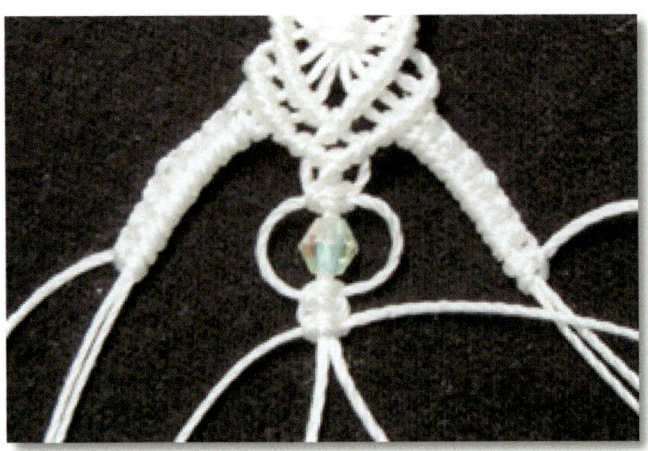

17. Separate 5-5. Take the outer cord on each side and tie a VLH knot around the other 4 cords. Now put all the cords together and tie a flat knot with the outer 2 cords, bending the VLH knot sections to form an arc.

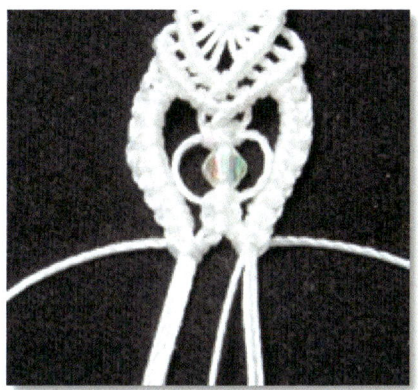 

18. Place the cross right-side up, then flip it over. Put the 8 center cords through a jump ring. Bring these cords straight down, then tie a flat knot with the two outer cords.

Glue, trim, and glue again.

Page 135

TIPS

- Keep the small baggies that you get from the bead store. These are mini zip tops that extra buttons (attached to clothes) also come in. Use it to fill with beads; either the oddly colored ones, or all the colors for a certain project. This makes storage is so much simpler! I can add several bags of beads to any one bead drawer. And when I want to use them, I can pull a few out of the bag at a time. The rest stay put and aren't rolling off my table. Now when I buy at the bead store, I am as happy about the little baggie they hand me as the beads themselves!

- Cut the ends of the cords at a slight angle for easier threading. Also when I am measuring cord for a pattern, I cut a little extra. That way if I need to trim the ends of a frayed cord to coax it thought a bead, I haven't sacrificed any project length.

- When you take C-Lon cord from a new spool, it will have a slight curl to it andyou may not need to straighten it. As you get further into the spool the curl intensifies and it will become necessary to iron the cords. Put your iron on the nylon setting (or set it to low or med-low). Take your cut cords and place them on the ironing board, then set the iron down on top of them. Gently pull all cords to the other side of the iron and you are done.

- If you are having a hard time getting the cord through a bead, you can use clear nail polish to strengthen the cord. This works well, but make sure it is not already a tight fit as the polish adds a little bulk to the cord.

- When I head to the store for beads, I take a bit of my C-Lon cord with me to color match. Place it in the previously mentioned mini baggie with any beads you already have for the project, and off you go.

- Keep the odds and ends from old pieces. Only 1 earring? Maybe that dangle can be a focal point for a bracelet or necklace. Ugly old necklace? Salvage the clasps before tossing it out.

Gallery

Here are a few of my other finished pieces. You can find the patterns at my website, **http://www.demure-designs.com**

Coral Necklace

Two Roads Diverged Bracelet

Ties That Bind Bracelet

Alluring Necklace

You might also like...

Learn How To Make Micro-Macramé Jewelry! Volume 1

Beginning Designs

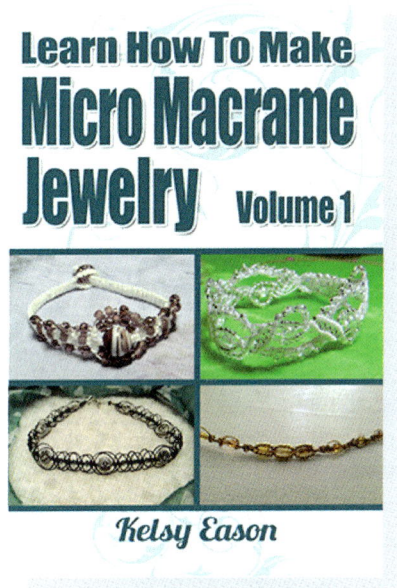

This illustrated guide teaches you step by step how to start making Micro Macrame jewelry. Written for the person with little to no knotting experience, this handbook walks you through the basic knots.

The first design is a straightforward bracelet using just one knot. This gives you the chance to get familiar with the cord and tension amounts. As you progress through each pattern, you will be introduced to a new knot or two, culminating in a final project which uses several knots.

Questions or Comments?

If you have any questions or comments about this book, I'd love to hear your thoughts. Email me at **info@demure-designs.com**

Facebook

If you want to follow me on Facebook, my Facebook page can be found here:

> http://www.facebook.com/DemureDesigns

Reviews

I'd really appreciate it if you left a review for the book on Amazon. Your experience with the book will help others decide if the book is useful enough to purchase.

Need More Patterns?

These aren't all the patterns I've created. If you need more patterns, take a moment to visit my website and see my latest creations. I'm constantly adding new patterns all the time. Sign up on my mailing list and I'll email you when I post a new pattern to the site. Visit my website here:

> **Demure Designs - www.demure-designs.com**

Printed in Great Britain
by Amazon